A furry marten peers down from a branch in a pine tree.

ANIMALS IN WINTER

by Ron Fisher

NATIONAL
GEOGRAPHIC
SOCIETY

Washington, D.C.

Brrr! The cold time of the year has come. Winter is here! A hare sits very still in the snow. The hare must find food and stay warm in winter. Winter is hard for many animals.

$\mathcal{S}$now covers the ground. Ice covers twigs and bushes that some animals eat. Food is hard to find. Not all animals look for food in the snow. Some sleep deeply in winter. This is called hibernation. Some move to warmer places where food is easier to find. This is called migration. Some make cozy homes and store food to eat in winter.

A deer does not hibernate or migrate long distances. It does not make a home or store food for the winter. The deer eats buds and twigs. It lies down to rest right in the snow. A thick winter coat helps keep the deer warm.

Bighorn sheep eat grass
and other plants. A male
bighorn, called a ram, paws
the snow to get at the plants.

Look closely at this tree.
A hungry moose has eaten
some of the bark. In winter,
moose also eat buds and twigs.
In summer, they like to eat
plants that grow in water.
But now the water is frozen.

These animals are called
pronghorns. They eat plants, too.
In winter, pronghorns move
to places where deep snow
does not cover the plants.

A mountain lion runs through a snowy forest. Its large paws are like snowshoes. They help the big cat move over the snow.

A weasel has caught a mouse. The weasel's white winter fur blends with the snow. The weasel can sneak up on mice and other animals that it eats.

Sniff! Sniff! A red fox pokes its nose deep into the cold snow. The fox has heard a mouse and is trying to catch it.

The snow does not keep these two hungry coyotes from looking for food.

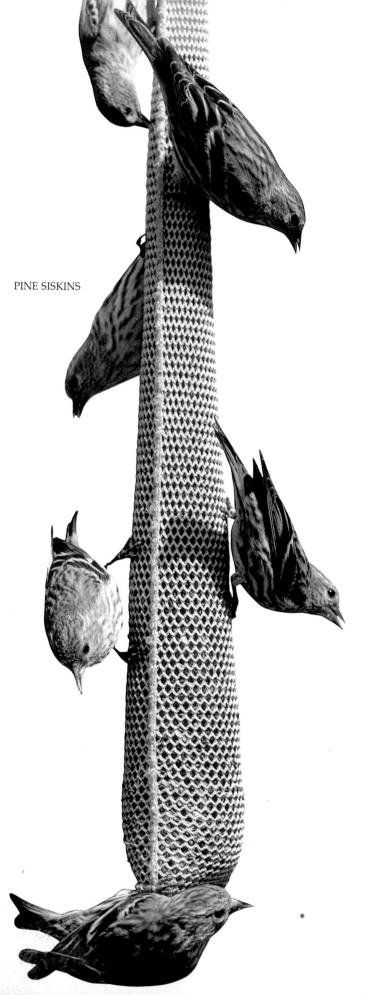

PINE SISKINS

Some people put food outside for animals in winter. Pine siskins, cardinals, blue jays, and other birds may come to your backyard if you put seeds and fruit out for them.

A squirrel eats
kernels of corn
at a feeder.
Sitting up,
it holds the food
in its paws.

CARDINAL

BLUE JAY

Beavers have built a house called a lodge in this stream.
When ice covers the water, the beaver family usually stays inside.
The beavers eat bark from twigs they have stored underwater.
When the stream isn't frozen, they can come outside to eat.

A squirrel is living
in the hollow trunk of a tree.
A woodpecker made the hole.
The squirrel will be snug
here during the winter.

This pika will be ready
when winter comes.
The pika stores food it will eat
while the snow falls.
It gathers leaves and stems,
then puts them on rocks
near its home. They dry out
in the sun. Later the pika
will pile the dried plants
beneath the rocks.

The pika has a round body,
with short legs and ears.
Thick fur helps keep it warm.
The little pika even has fur
on the bottoms of its feet!

PIKA (say PEA-kuh or PIE-kuh)

A prairie dog comes out of its burrow on a warm winter day. Prairie dogs stay underground in bad weather.

Shhh! A ground squirrel is fast asleep in its nest. It is hibernating. It eats a lot during the summer and gets very fat. Then it curls up in a ball and goes to sleep. The animal breathes more slowly, and its heart beats more slowly. Its body temperature drops. The ground squirrel lives off its body fat until spring.

Bears are lazy in winter. They sleep and sleep and sleep. But on nice warm days they may wake up. When bears leave their dens, they sometimes sniff and scratch trees. Then they may look for food. Bears eat insects, small animals, and birds' eggs. They eat roots, berries, nuts, and honey. They eat almost anything.

During the winter, the baby bears, called cubs, are born. In spring, they go outside with their mother. The cubs stay close to her. She shows them how to hunt for food.

$\mathbb{A}$nimals with
white coats are hard
to see in the white
snow. White coats help
some animals hide.
They help others hunt.

Polar bears are good swimmers. They live far in the north, where there
is snow and ice almost all the time. The bears look like big chunks
of ice. Their white coats help them sneak up on the animals they eat.
A baby harp seal has white fur for only the first few weeks
of its life, when it stays on the ice. Its fur will turn darker
before the seal begins to swim and find food in the ocean.

A snowshoe hare does not look the same in winter as it does in summer. In winter it has white fur. In summer it has brown fur. A white coat is hard to see in winter. A brown coat is hard to see in summer. The enemies of the hares have trouble finding them.

PTARMIGAN (say TAR-mih-gun)

Birds called ptarmigans change color, too. As summer ends, a ptarmigan begins to lose its brown feathers. It grows new white ones. This change is called molting. It happens every year. The ptarmigan becomes as white as the snow. This helps protect the bird from its enemies. In the spring, it grows brown feathers again.

Warm weather
is here at last.
Flowers are blooming.
The sun feels warm,
and the breeze feels
fresh. A young deer
called a fawn has
a spotted coat that
blends with flowers.
In late summer,
the fawn will grow
a gray coat like
its mother's.

ELK

MOUNTAIN GOAT

In spring, some animals molt. They lose their heavy winter coats and
grow lighter summer ones. A bull elk is growing a new summer coat.
It will be a pretty reddish color. His new antlers are covered
with soft skin called velvet. They will grow all summer long.
A mountain goat sheds his winter coat. Big clumps of hair fall off.

A watchful mother sheep
and her newborn baby
rest on a mountainside.
The lamb is only
a few days old.
During the summer
it will grow.
It will nibble grass
and other plants.
It will play in the sun
with other lambs.
It will leap from rock to rock
and climb near the cliffs
where it lives. The lamb
will begin to grow horns.
It will be bigger and stronger
before winter comes again.

MORE ABOUT

Animals in Winter

Winter can be a time of privation and suffering for wildlife. In the northern part of the United States and Canada, when cold winds howl and snow blankets the ground, many wild animals face a season of hardship. Finding food and shelter may become a matter of life or death.

Animals adapt to winter conditions in a variety of ways. Some animals—especially many kinds of birds—migrate.

A few kinds of mammals hibernate. Most of them curl up in burrows and sleep deeply through the winter. In a hibernating ground squirrel (18-19)*, body temperature is much lower than normal; breathing and

heart rates are extremely slow.

Some animals sleep for most of the winter, but their body temperatures do not drop sharply. Bears (20-21), for instance, usually go into their dens in the fall and stay there, sleeping off and on until spring. If disturbed, they can wake up quickly.

Some animals store food for the winter. Working feverishly during summer and autumn, pikas (17), beavers (14-15), and most squirrels (16) amass food that will see them through the cold months.

Other animals find food as best they can. Bighorn sheep (6-7) paw through snow for plants underneath, and deer (5) eat twigs and buds from shrubs and saplings.

Some birds glean insect eggs from bark or from the wood beneath. Weasels and foxes (10) sometimes catch small animals after hearing them under the snow.

Snowshoe hares (2-3) are sometimes aided in their quest for food by the snow itself. As the snow becomes deeper and deeper, a hare can nibble bark and twigs that it could not reach when the ground was bare.

Many animals grow thick coats that help keep them warm in winter. A deer's winter coat consists of long, stiff guard hairs and short, fine underfur (5). The underfur holds heat next to the deer's body much as fluffy down holds heat for a bird.

*Numbers refer to pages in *Animals in Winter*.

Resting but alert, a buck beds down in the snow. A thick coat, grown especially for winter, keeps the deer warm.

Snug in its den, a black bear awakes from its winter slumber.

Emerging from its burrow, a prairie dog looks around. Though not a true hibernator, it stays underground during severe winter weather.

Some animals do not build homes for the winter but lie down to rest right in the snow. Deer (5) usually try to find sheltered spots in swamps or thickets. Snowshoe hares (2-3) often crouch under snow-covered branches. Bears (20-21) find caves, hollow trees, or spots under the roots of over-turned trees.

Other animals build homes. Tree squirrels (16), for example, often leave their summer nests in tree branches and make winter nests inside hollow trees. There they remain snug even when the weather is stormy or cold.

Perhaps the most amazing home-builders are beavers (14-15). They construct dome-shaped lodges in ponds and streams. The lodges are built mainly of sticks and logs, which the beavers plaster with mud. This helps keep out the cold winter air while the beaver family eats and sleeps inside. The beavers never plaster the center parts of the lodge roofs; they leave them unsealed so that air can enter and escape. On cold winter days, you may see vapor rising from the tops of the lodges.

Winter may sometimes seem a cruel time for animals in the wild. But nature has provided most of them with effective adaptations for survival.

As winter ends, new life begins: Only a few days old, a Dall's sheep rests with its mother on a mountain slope.

The text by Ron Fisher was prepared with input from scientific consultants Dr. Richard W. Coles, Director, Washington University Tyson Research Center and Dr. Henry W. Setzer, Curator of Mammals, Emeritus, Smithsonian Institution. Educational consultants Dr. Glenn O. Blough and Judith Hobart and reading consultant Dr. Lynda Bush also provided helpful comments and suggestions. Original research was provided by Palmer Graham. Prior to paperback publication, the National Geographic Society reviewed the book to ensure its accuracy in light of current information and study.

The photographs were selected by the National Geographic Society's illustrations editor Charles E. Herron.
Credits: Stephen J. Krasemann, DRK PHOTO (cover, 4, 8-9, 10 lower, 28-29); Leonard Lee Rue III, ANIMALS ANIMALS (1,5); Mark Tomalty, MASTERFILE (2-3, 16); David C. Fritts, ANIMALS ANIMALS (6-7 upper, 24 upper left); Harry Engels (6-7 lower, 7, 17 upper, 17 lower, 26 left); Wayne Lankinen (10 upper); Annie Griffiths (11); Jen and Des Bartlett, BRUCE COLEMAN INC. (13 upper left); S. Osolinski, FREELANCE PHOTOGRAPHERS GUILD (12-13); National Geographic Photographer Bates Littlehales (12); Laura Riley, BRUCE COLEMAN INC. (13 upper right); Wolfgang Bayer, BRUCE COLEMAN INC. (14 lower left); Harry Engels, NATIONAL AUDUBON SOCIETY COLLECTION/PHOTO RESEARCHERS, INC. (14 lower right); John L. Ebeling (14-15); Jeff Foott, BRUCE COLEMAN INC. (18-19); S.C. Kaufman, NASC/PR (19); J. Van Wormer, BRUCE COLEMAN INC. (20-21); Wayne Lankinen, DRK PHOTO (21 upper); Stephen J. Krasemann, PETER ARNOLD, INC. (21 lower); Janet Foster, MASTERFILE (22); MASTERFILE (22-23); Ray Richardson, ANIMALS ANIMALS (24 lower left); Brian Milne, ANIMALS ANIMALS (24 right); Stephen J. Krasemann, BRUCE COLEMAN INC. (24-25); Kenneth W. Fink, BRUCE COLEMAN INC. (26 right); Tom and Pat Leeson (26-27); Leonard Lee Rue III, ANIMALS ANIMALS (30); Wayne Lankinen DRK PHOTO (31 upper left); S.C. Kaufman, NATIONAL AUDUBON SOCIETY COLLECTION/PHOTO RESEARCHERS, INC. (31 upper right); Stephen Krasemann, DRK PHOTO (31 lower); Jim Brandenburg (32).

This is prairie dog town, but where are all the prairie dogs? They are underground. They stay there while the snow piles high above them.

COVER: A spruce cone makes a mouthful for a red squirrel. The squirrel will eat the seeds inside it.

Library of Congress ℗ Data
Fisher, Ronald M.
  Animals in winter.
  (Books for young explorers)
  Summary: Describes how animals face the rigors of winter by hibernating, migrating, storing food, or changing colors to blend with the winter landscape.
  1. Animals—Wintering—Juvenile literature. [1. Animals—Habits and behavior. 2. Winter]
I. Title. II. Series.
QL753.F55 1982   591.5'43   82-47859
ISBN 0-87044-453-0
Kids Want to Know paperback printing ISBN 0-7922-3601-7